EMOTIONS

15 BIG feelings for littles

I0626089

It's okay to feel your feelings

Helping little ones navigate their emotional rollercoaster is vital for building self-awareness and emotional intelligence. This lively picture book uses everyday situations, simple language, and catchy rhymes to label feelings and model healthy coping strategies.

Copyright © [2023] by The Cheekyprimate

All rights reserved. No part of this book may be reproduced or transmitted in any form or by any means, electronic or mechanical, including photocopying, recording, or by any information storage and retrieval system, without written permission from the author, except for the inclusion of brief quotations in a review.

For my precious Kamsi.
In laughter. love. and hugs so tight
Our bond is firm. cherished and clear.
May these pages spark joy sincere.
Guiding you forward. year after year.

In this book, you'll find

15 BIG EMOTIONS
"FEELINGS" RHYME
MOOD CHART
HELPFUL TIPS

April is very

HAPPY

Eating strawberry cake
makes her feel so good
and giggly!

Oh no!

Alex dropped his ice cream cone!

And that made him feel

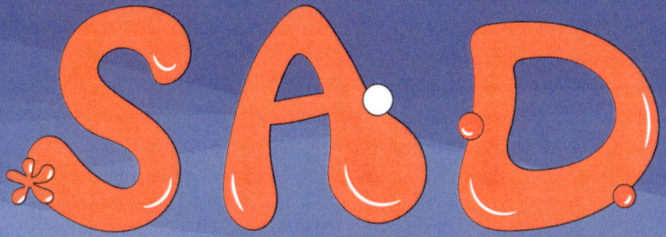

Morty is feeling

ANGRY*

He can't fit his puzzle
pieces together!

What's inside
the box?

WOW!!!

It's a gift!

Stella is so

SURPRISED

The fireworks went
Bang! Bang! Bang!!!

It made Andy very

SCARED

Yucky!

That tastes FUNNY!

Sally looks

DISGUSTED

Tito went to the park with Dad.

He had fun riding his bike!

Now, he's so

TIRED

Kamsi had a veggie snack.

He finished
EVERYTHING on his plate!

He felt really

PROUD

of himself.

Tara gives her teddy bear LOTS of SQUISHY hugs!

That's because she **LOVES** her teddy bear so much!

THIS OR THAT

Amy can only have ONE!

She is so

CONFUSED.

Abby gets
HUNGRY

EVERYTIME she thinks about pizza!

Zack likes dressing on his own.

But tying his shoelaces is hard!

It makes him feel

FRUSTRATED

GUESS what?

Zizi is going to the zoo today!

She is very

EXCITED

Mike likes playing fetch with his dog.

Playing alone makes him feel
LONELY

Vanessa loves her little brother
very much.

She is

THANKFUL

for him!

Happy, happy, jump and clap,
Turn around,
do a giggly dance!

If you're feeling
kinda blue,
Hug a friend,
they're here for you.

Surprises happen,
big and small,
Cherish them all, have a ball!

Sometimes angry, that's okay,
Take a deep breath,
it'll fade away.

Fear might come, and that's ok,
Hold my hand,
we'll work it out.

Little steps or big, it's true,
You shine bright
in all you do.

The moon is out,
rest your little head,
Snuggle up, it's time for bed.

Listen to your feelings, it's okay
"I don't like that,"
you're free to say.

Love is warm, like a sunny day,
Hug your teddy,
a squishy squeeze.

Tummy rumbles, time to eat,
Pizza, carrots,
a tasty treat.

When you're confused, take a break,
Ask for help,
it's a piece of cake.

Deep breath in,
and count to three,
Try again, a better way.

Excitement's like a happy dance,
Wiggle and giggle,
then spin around.

A smile from a friend,
a hand to hold,
Look around, you're not alone.

Thankful, thankful,
a happy heart,
For every little, lovely part.

MO

OD CHART

Tips to help you make the most of this book and navigate the emotional rollercoaster of toddler years.

STRATEGY	TIP	WHAT YOU CAN SAY:
Name Those Feelings	Use simple words to identify emotions.	Are you feeling frustrated because the puzzle pieces won't fit? It's okay, we can try again.
Express Yours Too	Be a feeling role model.	Mommy feels excited about our playdate too!
Read Together	Read the feelings rhymes in this book together.	Alex is feeling sad. Can you make a sad face like Alex?
Mood Chart	Use the mood chart pages in this book to label feelings.	How are you feeling today?
Use Daily Routines	Emotions can pop up during routines.	Uh-oh, did you spill some milk? It's okay, accidents happen. Let's clean up together!
Celebrate Small Achievements	Praise efforts and emotions.	You shared your toys! That's so kind and makes Mommy proud!
Music and Movement	Use music to express emotions.	Let's dance like we're happy! Can you dance like you're feeling silly too?
Create a Calm Corner	Have a quiet space for calming down.	When we feel mad, we can take a break in our cozy corner with a soft pillow.

Remember, toddlers are learning about their feelings just like they're learning to walk and talk. Your love, patience, and understanding are the best tools to guide them through this wonderful journey!

SCAN HERE

Share Your Thoughts on this Book!

Your opinion is incredibly valuable to me, and I would be thrilled if you could leave a review.

Also, don't forget to scan the QR code above to stay connected for more exciting content and updates!

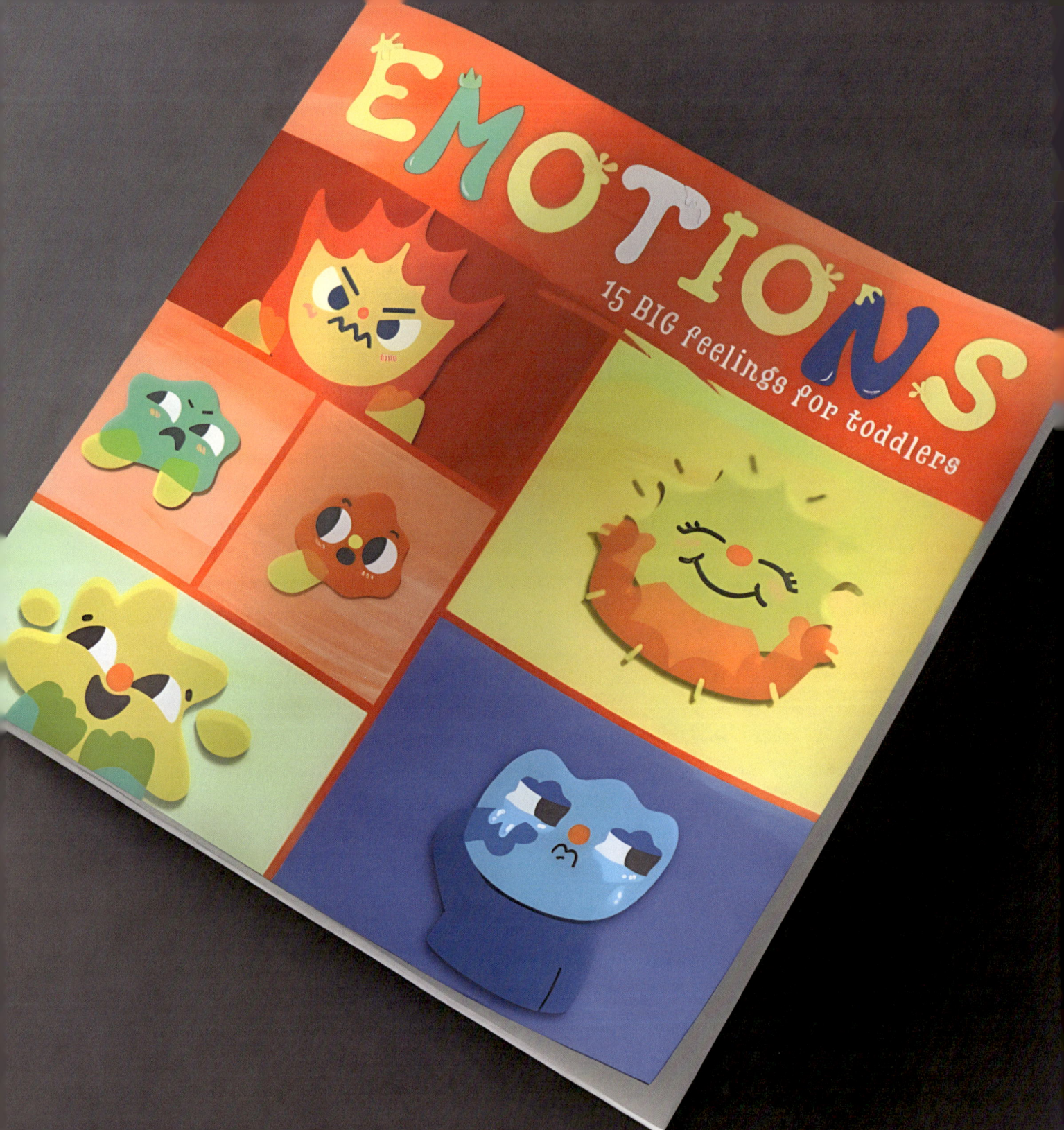

www.ingramcontent.com/pod-product-compliance
Lightning Source LLC
Chambersburg PA
CBRC090829120626
46547CB00008B/631

9 781998 368075